BLACK and WHITE
Animals

Giant Pandas

by Mari Schuh

CAPSTONE PRESS
a capstone imprint

Little Pebble is published by Capstone Press,
1710 Roe Crest Drive, North Mankato, Minnesota 56003
www.mycapstone.com

Library of Congress Cataloging-in-Publication Data
Names: Schuh, Mari C., 1975- author.
Title: Giant pandas / by Mari Schuh.
Description: North Mankato, Minnesota : Capstone Press, [2017] | Series:
    Little pebble. Black and white animals | Audience: Ages 6 to 8. |
    Audience: Grades K to grade 3. | Includes bibliographical references and
    index.
Identifiers: LCCN 2016019268| ISBN 9781515733720 (library binding) | ISBN
    9781515733911 (pbk.) | ISBN 9781515733959 (eBook PDF)
Subjects: LCSH: Giant panda—Juvenile literature.
Classification: LCC QL737.C27 S353 2017 | DDC 599.789—dc23
LC record available at https://lccn.loc.gov/2016019268

Editorial Credits
Gena Chester, editor; Kayla Rossow, designer; Morgan Walters, media researcher;
Kathy McColley, production specialist

Photo Credits
Minden Pictures: Bill Coster, 19; Newscom: Mitsuaki Iwago/ Minden Pictures, 15; Shutterstock:
Curly Pat, design element cover, Hung Chung Chih, backcover, 5, 7, 13, 17, 21, Lee Yiu Tung, 1, 11,
leungchopan, Cover, Markovka, design element throughout, Volt Collection, 9

Printed and Bound in China.
009958S17

Table of Contents

In the Forest

What's in the tree?

It's a panda!

Pandas live in China.

They live alone.

Pandas live in forests
on mountains.
The forests are cool and wet.

Pandas have a thick coat.

It is woolly.

It keeps pandas warm.

Daily Life

Pandas eat bamboo.

It is a tall grass.

It is hard.

Pandas have wide, flat teeth.
They crush bamboo.

Pandas eat a lot.
They eat for 12 hours
or more each day.
They sit and munch.

Pandas are strong.

They can swim.

They get away from danger
such as snow leopards.

Pandas climb.

They find a spot to rest.

Time for a nap!

Glossary

bamboo—a tall grass with a hard, hollow stem

China—a large country in eastern Asia

forest—a large area covered with trees and plants

mountain—an area of land that rises high above the land around it; mountains are taller than hills

snow leopard—a large cat that has grey fur and dark spots

woolly—soft and thick

Read More

Franks, Katie. *Pandas.* The Zoo's Who's Who. New York: PowerKids Press, 2015.

Peterson, Megan Cooley. *Giant Pandas are Awesome.* Awesome Asian Animals. North Mankato, Minn.: Capstone Press, 2016.

Schuetz, Kari. *Giant Pandas.* Animal Safari. Minneapolis: Bellwether Media, 2012.

Internet Sites

FactHound offers a safe, fun way to find internet sites related to this book. All of the sites on FactHound have been researched by our staff.

Here's all you do:
Visit *www.facthound.com*
Type in this code: 9781515733720

Check out projects, games and lots more at
www.capstonekids.com

Critical Thinking Using the Common Core

1. What body part helps pandas eat?
   (Key Ideas and Details)

2. Why do you think pandas eat a lot?
   (Integration of Knowledge and Ideas)

3. A panda's coat is woolly. What does "woolly" mean?
   (Craft and Structure)

Index